T0193539

Thamaso Ma Jyothirgamaya

A Novel & Unique Christian Perspective ● K. J. Oommen, MD, FAAN, FAES, FACNS

Copyright © 2019 K. J. Oommen, MD, FAAN, FAES, FACNS.

All rights reserved. No part of this book may be used or reproduced by any means, graphic, electronic, or mechanical, including photocopying, recording, taping or by any information storage retrieval system without the written permission of the author except in the case of brief quotations embodied in critical articles and reviews.

Scripture quotations are taken from The Holy Bible, New International Version®, NIV® Copyright © 1973, 1978, 1984, 2011 by Biblica, Inc.® Used by permission. All rights reserved worldwide.

Inspiring Voices books may be ordered through booksellers or by contacting:

Inspiring Voices
1663 Liberty Drive
Bloomington, IN 47403
www.inspiringvoices.com
1 (866) 697-5313

Because of the dynamic nature of the Internet, any web addresses or links contained in this book may have changed since publication and may no longer be valid. The views expressed in this work are solely those of the author and do not necessarily reflect the views of the publisher, and the publisher hereby disclaims any responsibility for them.

This book is a work of non-fiction. Unless otherwise noted, the author and the publisher make no explicit guarantees as to the accuracy of the information contained in this book and in some cases, names of people and places have been altered to protect their privacy.

Any people depicted in stock imagery provided by Getty Images are models, and such images are being used for illustrative purposes only. Certain stock imagery © Getty Images.

ISBN: 978-1-4624-1261-7 (sc)
ISBN: 978-1-4624-1262-4 (e)

Print information available on the last page.

Inspiring Voices rev. date: 02/24/2022

InspiringVoices®

DEDICATION

This monograph is dedicated to my mother, who was the embodiment of peace, grace and love.

WITH A FOREWORD BY

Rt. Rev. Dr. Isaac Mar Philoxenos, Diocesan Bishop
Diocese of North America and Europe

The Diocese Of North America & Europe
The Mar Thoma Church

Rt. Rev. Dr. Isaac Mar Philoxenos
Diocesan Bishop

It is with great pleasure that I write this foreword to Dr. K. J. Oommen's monograph *"Thamaso Ma Jyothirgamaya"*. As he indicated in chapter 2, I was surprised to see how his unique analysis of the Shanthi Manthra by the writers of the Upnishads fits his idea that the supplications of the shloka, used extensively in Hindu rituals, as a prayer or invocation to ॐ (Aum or Ohm), often interpreted as the 'trimurthy' of Brahma, Vishnu and Shiva, was granted by Jesus.

In Jesus one finds the form of Trinity. Truly he is the Son of God, born without a woman at the beginning of time and from a woman without a man at the appointed time, over 2000 years ago, who came into this world, for the singular purpose of bringing truth (sathya), light (jyothi) and gave us all the promise of everlasting life (amruthya) by his own death (mruthyu) and brought us peace.

I do hope this book will give new insight to the readers in the understanding of God in a different religious setting and it will also help the Christian community to engage in greater scrutiny of our own behavior in the environment we live in and ask ourselves whether we are living as emulators of Christ and whether we are truly reflecting Christ in our daily life in these perilous times.

I wish and pray that this book shall open the horizon of knowing others and deepen the quest to share the joy and peace one experiences. It also calls to fulfill the mandate of Jesus' great commission to his disciples to "Go to the ends of the earth to proclaim the Gospel" and bring the peace (shanthi) of God.

I appreciate the efforts of Dr. K. J. Oommen in bringing out of this piece of literary work that gives new impetus in our understanding of God and the world.

May the God of peace give grace to overcome the forces of death and decay with the power of light and life and let the divine in every individual be rekindled to radiate light that removes darkness.

Wishing everyone peace and blessings,

Signed
Rt. Rev. Dr. Isaac Mar Philoxenos

INTRODUCTION

Most people do not read or pay attention to the introduction to a book. I have found it very useful to carefully read the introduction of a book and I do encourage whoever picks up this book, particularly the Christian readers, to do the same. Before I get into my reasons to routinely read introductions, an important item I like to bring to the attention of the readers at the very outset is that to spell Hindi and Sanskrit words, which I have used in this book, I have chosen to use a phonetically closer form of spelling than some of their Anglicized versions currently in use in the English literature. When such Anglicized words are available, they are placed in parentheses next to the ones I chose to use. Now let me go over some reasons as to why I recommend reading introductions to the books we read.

First, a well-written introductory piece, should familiarize the reader to the background and the reason(s) for the author writing it and his or her inspiration for the endeavor. It orients the reader to the theme of the book giving him or her a deeper insight into what the book is about and thus a better understanding of its message. It will help ward off any unnecessary bias, which the title or the appearance of the book may elicit in the mind of the reader as well. In some cases, however, the author may want to keep some surprises, as I have done in this case, but only to the end of the first chapter of this book. The contents of the following paragraphs should give the reader plenty of hints, nonetheless. The second reason is particularly relevant to this book and that is the fact that this book is expected to reach people across cultures, belief systems and philosophical and ideological perspectives. Because individual expectations differ greatly from various cultural points of view, and because those who expect a certain stream of thought from this book may find some ideas or some of the statements in this book contradictory to its message, I believe it is imperative that I should remind the reader that one must keep an open mind until the end. Let me assure you, that if you do so, you will find that the goal of this book is singular and its purpose straightforward, which is to convey the message that the light that shines and reveals the truth about life; that is life everlasting, the assurance of which shall bring peace to the world, and which a glorious civilization craved for close to three thousand years through a very special incantation by its sages, has been hidden from our eyes and that the world and all its pundits missed it for centuries. One of the most important goals of this book is to expose this fact and the irony that the very group of people who are reflecting that light and revealing that mystery are the ones who are suffering persecution in the hands of those whom they are trying to enlighten.

In 2012, I was at a professional conference at the Bolgatti Palace in Kochi, Kerala, India, during the course of which I was invited for an evening reception. At the start of the reception, there was a brief ceremony where a special lamp was lighted. This lamp is germane to the Indian subcontinent, particularly South India, and is known as "nilavilakku". As the lamp was being lit by the then Medical Director of the Amrita Hospital in Kochi, there was a recitation of a "shlokam" (song) which those who live in India are very familiar with. It is as commonly used in the beginning of

Hindu religious functions as the Indian National Anthem, (Janaganamana) is used at the end of most ceremonial occasions by patriotic Indians. It was a "Shanthi Manthra" (Shanti Mantra) which will hereinafter be spelled as such, because the former is phonetically closer to its pronunciation than the latter, its Anglicized counterpart, common in English usage. It is the most popular of the several such manthras (mantras) in the Vedās and became the inspiration for this book, because of the sudden realization of its true meaning that I had on that occasion.

I am sure many of you have had such moments in life, when something or some idea suddenly strikes you like it did Shri Budha while meditating under the "Bodhi" tree. Such moments of "bodhodaya", or enlightenment, wherein that realization becomes a passion, is very much like a "Eureka" or "Ah Ha" moment, which then drives one to action either to prove it or disprove it. Such moments are extremely gratifying and empowering. This was such a moment for me, and I decided to study it in more detail. The more I studied it, the more I became convinced of its veracity and I believe the time has come for me to share it with the rest of the world.

Some of my Christian friends take offence to Christians participating in ceremonies where Hindu traditions are observed, as was the one I participated in, in Kochi. Yes, I realize, that I may be considered guilty of it by some of my friends. Those Christians who are familiar with what the lamp itself represents may take issue with a Christian lighting such a lamp, let alone participating in such functions, because for Hindus, the base of the lamp represents Brahma, (The creator) its stem Vishnu (The protector) and its top Shiva (The destroyer), the three important deities of the religion. It is not my intent to go into further details of what the lamp and its various parts represent, nor into an in-depth analysis of what its lighting bestows on the believers by its powers. Suffice it to say that when one looks at what the lamp represents for the Hindu people, such an act as lighting the nilavilakku itself may be construed as a veneration of the Hindu trinity and thus anathema to the puritans among the Christians. But it is extremely important for my Christian readers to understand that what the lamp signifies for my Hindu audience is not what is being celebrated here, but rather the Shanthi Manthra and its meaning are the subjects of this book. I simply want my Christian friends to understand that this book is not what the lamp is about or its veneration, but that it is about a unique interpretation of the Shanthi Manthra, which incidentally, yet symbolically is chanted corresponding to the lighting of the lamp. I am compelled to share this idea, this revelation that I had, while listening to that shlokam on that particular occasion in Kochi, with my Christian friends, because I believe that it is a powerful tool to bring the Good News about Jesus to a Hindu Nation and its people.

Exodus 23:24 clearly prohibited the Israelites from venerating other gods when it admonished them to "Do not bow down before their gods or worship them or follow their practices". However, we also know that Naaman, the commander of the King of Aram, who spilled much Israelite blood, was not denied healing by Elisha as he came to him for the cure of his leprosy. Further, after he was healed of his illness by following the instructions of Elisha, albeit reluctantly and only because of the urging of his own servants, he, after having realized that the God of Israel was the only true God, and having made the phenomenal plan to carry two mules' load of earth from Israel to build and an altar for Yahweh (the God of Israel) in his homeland, makes a very unique request for one exception to be granted to him by the prophet, as recorded in 2 Kings 5:18. There we see that he requests Elisha "18 But may the Lord forgive your servant for this one thing: When my master enters the temple of Rimmon (his king's temple), to bow down and he is leaning on my arm and I have to bow there also—when I bow down in the temple of Rimmon, may the Lord forgive your servant for this." Thereafter we see that the man of God (Elisha), in the following verse (2 Kings 5:19) instead of rebuking him, blesses him and sends him on his journey back home, by telling him: "Go in peace".

Elisha does not condone Naaman's rationalizations, nor does he offer him a Talmudic list to observe, once he is back in Syria. Neither did he crush the Syrian neophyte's faith by placing a burden Elisha knew could prove fatal to him. Elisha did not cause him to be bruised by Naaman's master nor cause his life to be snuffed out, once he is back with his master doing the rituals for his master's pagan gods in Syria. Here Elisha does something very Jesusesque! (I know, I am introducing a new word here). It was similar to what we read in Matthew 12:20; "A bruised reed he will not break, and a smoldering wick he will not snuff out". Elisha made Naaman's burden light. Elisha did not place a yoke on Naaman that would have been too heavy for him, as if Elisha's action was a premonition of Matthew 11:30; "30 For my yoke is easy and my burden is light." Elisha did what Jesus would have done!

Further in Acts 15:1-21, we read a very instructive story about how some from Judea came to Antioch and taught that all new believers in Christ should be circumcised to be saved. Apostle Paul who began to convert non-Jews to the faith had issue with this teaching and a dispute arose over whether the new converts had to follow the old Jewish religious laws, in particular whether the males needed to be circumcised. At some point, possibly in 48 AD, Paul traveled to Jerusalem with Barnabas and some others to get the advice of the apostles and elders on the matter and to try and resolve the issue. In that gathering of what may be called the first "Ecumenical Council of the Apostles", Apostle Peter narrated the dream he had in Joppa to the whole group and supported Paul's position. James the Just, the brother of Jesus and the Bishop of Jerusalem, made a very insightful statement at the conclusion of the meeting to all who were gathered as we read in Acts 15:19 and 20, that "19 It is my judgment, therefore, that we should not make it difficult for the Gentiles who are turning to God. 20 Instead we should write to them, telling them to abstain from food polluted by idols, from sexual immorality, from the meat of strangled animals and from blood." This was a minimalistic approach, which covered the essentials rather than lay down a comprehensive set of rules, which would have been difficult to enforce. The point being that we must make it easy for those who want to reach out to the Hindu people by lighting a nilavilakku, to do so, because we sure can light it without worshipping it. A puritanical approach by questioning the practice and forbidding the tradition may only help to bruise the cause of Christianity and snuff out the faith of the novice.

Be that as it may, let me emphasize again that this book is not a veneration of the lamp itself, but of the meaning of its lighting. The symbolism of the lighting of the lamp removing the darkness is the theme of this book, and not the lamp itself. And that is a bridge to the other meanings that the Shanthi Manthra conveys, namely that Jesus is the truth and that He brought everlasting life to all the world, by his own death and left his peace with us before He returned to his Father!

Imagine the experience of Apostle Paul in the marketplace in Athens, the then capital of paganism and idol worship. As he took a walk daily in their marketplace, he came across an altar with an inscription "To an unknown god". Paul must have had a moment of enlightenment when he saw that altar, because while debating the Athenian scholars later in the Areopagus, he used that experience to tell them about that unknown god. In Acts 17:22 and 23 we read as follows; 22 Paul then stood up in the meeting of the Areopagus and said: "People of Athens! I see that in every way you are very religious. 23 For as I walked around and looked carefully at your objects of worship, I even found an altar with this inscription: to an unknown god. So, you are ignorant of the very thing you worship - and this is what I am going to proclaim to you." Paul's use of what he saw on the altar in his speech had a profound influence on his listeners on that day.

In the Shanthi Manthra of the Brhadaranyaka Upanishad (Brihadāranyaka Upaniṣhad), we have a powerful tool to effectively address our Hindu brothers and sisters, because the sole and single answer to the yearnings expressed in that shloka, came from none other than Jesus Christ! Unbeknownst to the masses that routinely and piously chant the manthra is the fact that Jesus is the light that came to remove the darkness of sin from this world, He is the truth that reveals Satan's lies, He is the one whose death brought eternal life to all and He is the prince of peace that left his peace that transcends all understanding with his beloved disciples to pass it on to us, the present generation, before he concluded his mission as a man on earth!

ॐ शान्तिः शान्तिः शान्तिः ॥

CHAPTER 1
The Hindu Kush

According to the purānas (ancient lore), the first man of the present Yuga and the first King of the country we call India today, was Manu who was svayambhuva (self-formed) according to one version, but was the son of Brahma, the creator, himself according to another. The Sanskrit word for man is "manu-gen", (one who is born of Manu) and hence the word "man" (mānava) owes its origin to Manu. Is it a coincidence that in the Bible too, the term used by his creator (Jehovah) for the first human was "man"? Was it because he was made out of clay by his hand (manus), the Latin word for hand, or is it because God himself spoke the Proto-Indo-European (PIE) language that included Latin and Sanskrit? Did God call the first of his creation Adam, as the Bible narrates in the story of creation in Genesis Chapter 1, because, as it is generally believed that "adamu" in Akkadian meant "to make" or because man was made from "adamah" which in Hebrew meant red clay, the latter referring to the (red) color of man? It makes equal or even more sense to believe that the root for Adam is the Sanskrit word "आदिम" (ādim) meaning prime or first – because he was the first! At this juncture I wonder if Sanskrit itself was the root of the PIE languages!

Taking the argument one step further, one can surmise that Sanskrit and its script are known as "Devanagari" (of the city of gods) for the simple reason that it was the language written and spoken by the gods. Is it possible that the "Creator" himself spoke that language (Sanskrit), because he was from a celestial city, as the Bible asserts?

Etymology and speculation aside, let us return to the purānas. Although Manu was the first king according to the puranās, before the British, Manu's country was known as Bhāratha after a later, yet legendary Indian king, "Bharatha"; its western region being well known to the ancients as Hindu Kush, which is now, in part, in Pakistan. The term Hindu is derived from Sindhu (Indus River) and was in use by the Greek from the time of Herodotus in the 5th Century BC. Much of the country's initial civilization flourished along the banks of the Indus river, known as the "Indus Valley". Popularized by the British, "India" became the best-known name for this ancient land.

The peace-loving sages of Bhāratha were responsible for the creation of the Vedās and the Upanishads or the Vedānthas, so called because the latter form the "end" of the "Vedās". Arthur Schopenhauer, a German philosopher was deeply impressed by the Upanishads and called it "the production of the highest human wisdom". These compendia of ancient words of wisdom by their creators demonstrate their knowledge, piety, morals as well as their literary prowess. Legend has it that the Vedās would have been lost in the Pralaya (The Great Flood), if Manu and the Saptharshies (Sapta-rishies) who created the books, were not saved by Vishnu by his first incarnation as Matsya (fish). See Image 1, below.

1

(Image used with permission of Gorakhpur Gita Press, Uttar Pradesh, India)

Image 1, Matsya saving Manu and the Saptharshies During the Pralaya

According to the Puranās, during the reign of Manu, Vishnu (The Protector) who knew of an impending flood that would destroy every living animal and plant, came to Manu in the form of a tiny fish while he was washing his hands in a river, and offered to save him if he would save its life form other predatory fishes in the river. Manu agreed. Eventually before the flood came, the fish instructed Manu to build a boat to escape the flood and to take "all medicinal herbs, all the varieties of seeds and other animals" with him to repopulate the earth with plants and animals after the flood. Manu, accompanied by his family, the seven saints (Saptharshies) who carried the Vedās and Vasuki, the serpent, boarded the boat. Manu tied the boat to Matsya with Vasuki. The Matsya then pulled the boat with all of them in it to the top of the Malaya Mountains (Himavan) where it rested until the waters that turned the entire world into a single ocean receded after seven days and nights. Vishnu thus saved the Vedās and Manu then repopulated the earth with his children. This story is eerily similar to the Biblical account of Noah's Flood, which lasted longer, for forty days and forty nights, from which he and his family escaped with a pair each of all birds and animals by building a boat according to instructions he received from Jehovah, later releasing the birds and animals and repopulating the earth.

The Upanishads contain many manthras (mantras) or incantations, written for various purposes and occasions and the Shanthi Manthras are intended to be chants for peace. The title of this book is part of ancient India's most famous prayer, a four liner that is quoted below, and represents the spiritual yearnings of this great nation. It is the most popular "Shanthi Manthra" and is excerpted from the Brhadaranyaka Upanishad. It is used as a reverent prayer, chanted to bring peace through the divine blessings of enduring truth, everlasting light and eternal life to those who are gathered in the venue concerned. In recent times the Manthra was popularized by its use in the "Navras" soundtrack of the movie "The Matrix Revolutions", a 2003 science fiction action film, which was the conclusion of a trilogy, the storyline then being continued in "The Matrix Online" (MxO) a massively multiplayer online role playing game until 2009, when it was discontinued by Sony Entertainment.

The Shanthi Manthra, which I will be dealing with specifically for the purpose of this book, is as noted above, one of the most popular and best known and is quoted below in the Devanagari script:

"ॐ असतो मा सद्गमय ।
तमसो मा ज्योतिर्गमय ।
मृत्योर्मा अमृतं गमय ।
ॐ शान्तिः शान्तिः शान्तिः ॥"

If you grew up in India, you are no stranger to the above four lines of the manthra, because it is used as a prayer at the beginning of spiritual and religious gatherings, in schools as the morning session starts and prior to the opening of many social events and other solemn occasions. The chant is initiated with the symbolic lighting of a special multi-tiered oil lamp, generic to the Indian Subcontinent. The true essence of this manthra and its celestial fulfillment is what I like to convey through this book.

When and where the pleadings of this manthra were actually granted to the humankind, may come as a surprise to many. Many will embrace my analysis of the divine fulfilment of this sublime prayer. Some may brush it off as conjecture, and others will consider it controversial or plain heresy. But all who desire for peace and tranquility in this world, should agree that the true meaning of this ancient chant that summarizes the soul's desire of every human being, this ultimate prayer for peace, is more relevant today, because we live in such tumultuous times. Not only there is increasing religious persecution, but more political and racial unrest in parts of India now, than ever before. There seems to be no letting up of the condition in sight either.

Mother India welcomed wave after wave of immigrants and received them with open arms into her embrace from time immemorial. It has seen some powerful conquerors and kings along the way, but India has been a multi-tribal country for most of its existence, and the in-fights among the tribes helped the British establish their domination in India prior to its independence from them in 1947. When one looks at the current unrest, it seems like people have forgotten the history of our predicament of subjugation to a foreign power that resulted from such petty tribal conflicts.

Modern India was born because Bappuji (Mahatma Gandhi) shed the sweat of his brow to liberate her from the clutches of Imperial England, eventually shedding his own blood for India at the hand of a religious fanatic. Gandhiji's followers penned a secular constitution to lead her into the future. Times have changed. Today we see a different type of shedding of blood than Mahatma Gandhi's. What we see now is the kind of bloodshed espoused by the likes of Nathuram Godse, his assassin. Now, instead of religious tolerance, which our founding fathers etched into our nation's culture, we see the persecution against religion and peoples' right to freely choose and follow their spiritual calling or political affiliation. We see men and women being stabbed in the footpaths and sidewalks of our villages, beaten in the back alleys and byways of our towns, pulled out of their doorsteps and dragged along driveways and roadways of the cities of our once tolerant and amiable motherland, all because of their choice of an ideology other than that of those who bully them. As proof, we have seen abuse of Christian missionaries in the streets of India for trying to spread the Gospel. We have seen the vile and grotesque sight of an Australian missionary and his children being burned alive while sleeping in their vehicle in one of the highways of our once longsuffering and peaceful country. Even religious gatherings have seen massive stampedes that trample men, women and children to their death. To be fair, I have to add that this impatience and intolerance has not been religious alone. We have seen mobs in action for social and economic reasons as well, such as the senseless and barbaric killing of a destitute for stealing in Kerala, which we call "god's own country". These stories bear witness to a peace, which is slowly slipping away.

We need this chant (Shanthi Manthra) to ring its sweet melody, now, not only in the country's corridors of power, its judicial edifices and the hallways of governmental offices, but also in private and public societal gathering places as well. We need this manthra to resonate in its villages, echo in its mountains and jungles and reverberate in its valleys, riverbanks, shores and beaches. One may say that we need this chant now more than ever before and that we need to recite it with renewed zeal, now that the unrest that was seen predominantly in the political arena has metastasized from there into the cultural and social spheres as well. At least it may seem so from the pervasive evil we hear about and the ghastly events we have been witnessing, because of intolerance!

Fret not, dearly beloved! The good news is that we have already received the answer to this prayer, a little more than two thousand years ago! You will know the name of that deity who came to this world for that purpose as you read on. We as a people need to cherish and promote that name above all names in our hearts now more than ever before. We need to practice his teachings with vigor, valor and a commitment, to bring us together, so that we may re-establish that elusive peace that seems to be slithering away from us and return India to its status as a neutral, secular, race blind nation and the "the land of peace" it once was.

CHAPTER 2
The Shanthi Manthra

This monograph is intended to remind all those who are yearning for peace and perspiring to remove darkness through the realization of truth, life and light in this world (which is the plea that constitutes the heart of this chant), that the prayer has been answered and the invocation for peace that it ends in, has been granted to us. What remains is for us to simply recognize the one who delivered on this prayer, believe and accept him for who he is. "How so?" One may ask! The answer is that if we simply open our eyes, we will see that truth, life, light and peace were already brought to this world by one man who came to this world, solely for that purpose, as if it were the answer to this chant and that this man himself was the embodiment of truth (sathya), life (amrutham), light (jyothi) and brought peace in to the midst of the chaos in this world. In the following chapters, I will attempt to explain this unique concept section by section, by using the lines of the Shanthi Manthra, quoted below.

"Asatho mā sadgamaya, thamaso mā jyotir gamaya, mrityor mā amritam gamaya, Oṁ śhānti śhānti śhāntiḥ." Line by line, it means the following.

> **Asatho mā sadgamaya** - From ignorance, lead me to truth;
> **Thamaso mā jyothir gamaya** - From darkness, lead me to light;
> **Mruthyor mā amrutam gamaya** - From death, lead me to immortality;
> **Oṁ śhānti śhānti śhāntiḥ** - Aum (Ohm) peace, peace, peace!

The word "ignorance" for "asatho" (asato) as translated above, I say, is arbitrary because it means much more. Asatho is better translated into "untruth", granted that the lack of knowledge of the truth surely is ignorance, but singularly of truth. In fact, it also refers to that which is non-existent and unreal and to the human pursuit of vanity. The next line is a supplication for our deliverance from thamas (the state of being lost to sin from goodness) and to keep us from the pursuit of evil by God's (light). That being the second line makes it no less important, but rather it is the central and most serene and profound of the three lines. Simply stated, it is a supplication to Aum (the Lord) to move us from "thamas" (tamas) or darkness, to light or clarity and most importantly to purity. In the same way, the choice of the word "immortality" for "amrutham" (amrita) in the third line, before the final invocation for "peace," is also arbitrary. Literally it is a prayer to Aum (the supernatural) to lead us from "mruthyu" (mrityu) or death to "amrutha" or ambrosia, the state of perennial or eternal life. In the fourth and the final line, the writer of Shanthi Manthra is exhorting the Aum (the supreme-being), the trinity, or the Holy Ghost (as in the Christian religion), or the Holy Word or the word of creation to bring peace into the midst of chaos.

The sum and substance of the prayer, thus, is to eliminate untruth, death and darkness (that which differentiates us, the mortals) from the immortal and to bring "shanthi" (peace) to us by shining the light (jyothi) on the truth (sathya) of our sinful nature and thereby to bring us eternal life (amrutham) and eventually, the transcendental and idyllic bliss of nirvana or the state of being one with godhead. The chant embodies the very spirit and bears testimony to the mental fabric of the ancient sages of our motherland. It embodies the quintessence of Indian culture. It is the soul (atman) of India, the land of peace. The four phrases of the chant have reverberated in the corridors of Indian history for at least 2700 years as the best estimates of the origin of the Upanishads, the parent compendium of this and many other Shanthi Manthras would suggest, as it dates back to 700 BC at the latest.

But what do these four lines truly mean? Who is the chant really appealing to? Who could be the object of this exhortation by the pundits (scholars) of ancient India? It is not specifically addressed to any of the 33 crores (330,000,000) of gods of the puranās. Many English translations by renowned Hindu Scholars simply use the word "Lord" (Paramaeswar) for the word Aum (Ohm), granted that other Hindu scholars interpret Aum as the Hindu trinity of Brahma, Vishnu and Shiva. Most importantly, who in heaven or earth can deliver this humanly impossible goal? Yes, I say impossible, as we only see glimpses of periods of such peace in history, if it ever existed, in the utopian times of Shangri-La, Rama Rajya and during the reign of Mahabali (Maveli) in the picturesque southern state of Kerala, all of which are merely legends at best. Perhaps we saw the semblance of an utopia in India, during the reign of the great king Ashoka, the legendary ruler of India who espoused ahimsa (non-violence) following the teachings of Shri Budha, whom some have considered (arguably) to be one of the incarnations of Vishnu himself.

Be ready to be surprised because in this unique analysis of the Manthra, I posit that this prayer made by the writers of the Upnishads to Aum, has already been granted by a God in human history. Yes, He came as a man to this world, for the sole purpose of delivering on this prayer. It is for all to see, nay, it is there only for those who have eyes to see, for all those who have ears to hear and for all those who have hearts to believe. Believe it or not, this prayer was already answered by one man who came to this world, for the singular purpose of bringing truth (sathya), shining his light (jyothi) on the untruth (asathya) and giving us life everlasting (amrutham) by his own death (mruthyu) and thereby bringing us peace.

Yes, Jesus was born as man and answered the prayers to Aum by the sages of ancient India who created the Upanishads. This legendary prayer, this sublime supplication that embodies the sum and substance of the morality of the Nation of India and the desire of the hearts of its fathers for peace has already been granted. He that carried out this task himself is the truth (sathya) who removed untruth (asathya) as he himself testified, "I am the truth, the way and the life". He himself is the living bread sent from heaven who gave us the living water and died for our sins and by his death (mruthyu) conferred everlasting life (amrutham) to all, after which he ascended into heaven leaving his peace with us. After fulfilling all three of the pleas (the first 3 lines of the chant), he left his earthly body, leaving his peace with us, a peace that "passeth all (human) understanding", not like the ephemeral and evanescent peace that the world gives us but as he (God) only can give. As he left us, after delivering on all three exhortations of the manthra by the writers of the Upanishads, his predestined mission, he left with the admonition to his disciples to "let not your hearts be troubled", to "believe in him" and to "not be afraid", entrusting his followers to pass that peace (shanthi) on to posterity.

Who is this man and what is the proof, you are sure to ask me. In this expose of the one who, I propose carried out this humanly impossible task, I like to deal with the first three lines in a different order, before I get to the last (fourth) line, the invocation for peace. First, I will discuss how he is the one who delivered us from darkness (thamas) and led us to light (jyothy). Then I will analyze how he disposed of our death and bought us eternal life (amrutham) by shedding his own blood and embracing his own death (mruthyu) on our behalf. Finally, in this discourse on the one who brought the passion of the ancient sages for peace to fruition, I will address how he led us from Satan's lie (asathyam) to the first man and woman on earth that brought death to mankind, to the everlasting truth (sathyam) and how he delivered us from eternal damnation. In conclusion, I will demonstrate how he, being the "prince of peace" brought peace (shanthi) on earth, and goodwill toward men by his birth as predicted by the prophets long before his birth and as proclaimed by the angels to his mother and father shortly before and to some shepherds soon after his birth.

CHAPTER 3
Thamaso Ma Jyothir Gamaya (From Darkness, Lead Me to Light)

There is no doubt that light removes darkness. Scientists tell us that darkness is the absence of light. It is true. The Bible has the proof. In the beginning, there was no light. Father God brought light into existence when he created light out of darkness at the dawn of time as is recorded in Genesis 1:1, 2. "1 In the beginning God created the heavens and the earth. 2 Now the earth was without form (nebulous) and void (empty), darkness (thamas) was over the surface of the deep, and the Spirit of God was hovering over the waters." The one who materialized the Shanthi Manthra, the Son of (God) was beside the Father in the moment of creation as recorded by John the Evangelist in John 1:2, 3. "2 He was with God (as he was from the beginning, part of the Triune God almighty). 3 Through him all things were made; without him nothing was made that has been made." Then, with his birth, Jesus brought light (jyothi) to the spiritual arena as we read in John 1:5 that "The light shines in the darkness, and the darkness has not overcome it." The world tried to remove that light (Jesus) by his crucifixion, but the world (evil) did not succeed. What more proof do we need that this man is the one who delivered on the prayer, the Shanthi Manthra, of the ancient sages of India? But there is more!

The very same time the Saptharshies who wrote the Upanishads were writing the Shanthi Manthra, the Biblical prophet Isaiah who lived in the 8th century BC, the same century the writers of the Upanishads lived in, foretold the coming of the one who by his birth, life and death would deliver on all that the ancient Indian rishies prayed for. In Isaiah 9:2, he states "The people that walked in darkness (thamas) have seen a great light: they that dwell in the land of the shadow of death, upon them hath the light (jyothi) shined." Proof that this was said about the same person that I propose did fulfill this aspect of the chant, is afforded in Matthew 4:16, "The people which sat in darkness (thamas) saw great light; and to them which sat in the region and shadow of death, light (jyothi) is sprung up", as he refers to Jesus' move from Nazareth to Capernaum, when Jesus heard about the imprisonment of John the Baptist. During his earthly ministry, as alluded to above, the one who delivered on the Shanthi Manthra, Jesus himself, said: "I am the light of the world. Whoever follows me will never walk in darkness (thamas) but will have the light (jyothi) of life" (John 8:12). Yes, these are Jesus' own words and a skeptic has every right to doubt one's testimony about oneself. But there are others who bore witness to the veracity of Jesus being the light (jyothi) sent from above to remove the darkness (thamas) in this world.

Image 2, Creation of Light

In the beginning God created the heavens and the earth. Now the earth was formless and empty, darkness was over the surface of the deep, and the Spirit of God was hovering over the waters. And God said, "Let there be light," and there was light. Genesis 1:1-3.

In Luke chapter 1, we read about the circumstances surrounding the birth of John the Baptist who was the messenger who was sent as the forerunner of Jesus. Zechariah, John's father, was an old man and his wife was also old beyond the age of conception when he received a promise from an angel of the Lord, of the birth of a son whom they both longed for. Because of his doubt about the promise he received, due to his and his wife's ages at which conception and childbearing were unthinkable for them and for anyone for that matter, he then became mute and remained so to everyone's bewilderment, for the term of Elizabeth's (his wife's) surprise pregnancy that occurred as he was promised. After the birth of his child, when it came to the naming of his son, Zechariah had to do it by writing on a tablet, because he was unable to speak. After the child's birth, narrated in Luke 1:76-79, we see that Zachariah, regained his ability to speak when he unexpectedly and again to the surprise of every one in his family wrote "John" on the tablet as the angel commanded him to do when he received the promise. As soon as Zechariah did this, his tongue was loosened and he was filled with the Holy Ghost and prophesied, saying, "76 And you, my child, will be called the prophet of the Most High; for you will go on before the Lord (Jesus) to prepare his way for him; 77 to give his people (Jews) the knowledge of salvation through the forgiveness of their sins, 78 because of the tender mercy of God, by which the rising sun (Jesus) will come to us from heaven 79 to shine on (shed light on = jyothi on) those living in darkness (thamas) and in the shadow of death (mruthyu), to guide our feet into the path of peace (shanthi)." In this passage Zechariah, points out that John, his son was the one to come before the light (jyothi) from heaven (Jesus) would.

Again, as his parents brought Jesus to the temple on the 40th day after his birth, for his consecration as required by Mosaic Law, we see there, an old man by the name of Simeon, who was eagerly waiting for the Messiah and had received a promise that he will not see death until he saw the one who was the deliverer of the Jews, as the prophets of the Old Testament had predicted, and for whom not only him but all the Jews were eagerly waiting for. As soon as Simeon beheld baby Jesus, he was miraculously moved by the Spirit and said this, as recorded by the Evangelist Luke, in Luke 2:29-32, "29 Sovereign Lord, as you have promised, you may now dismiss your servant in peace (shanthi). 30 For my eyes have seen your salvation (the Messiah), 31 which you have prepared in the sight of all nations: 32 a light (jyothi) for revelation to the Gentiles, and the glory of your people Israel". This prayer Simeon uttered on the spur of that moment has become known as the Canticle of Simeon. Simeon's testimony of baby Jesus being the light (jyothi) that came for the deliverance of the nation of Israel and to allow him to depart in peace from this world, is one of the prime examples of a spontaneous spiritual revelation of the true nature of Jesus, paralleled only by his own disciple Simon Peter's words as Jesus being the "Messiah, the Son of the living God", that we read in Matthew 16:16.

In the Book of John (the Apostle), in contradistinction to John (the Baptist), we see the confirmation of Zechariahs' prophesy about his son being the one to come before the Messiah (Jesus), by the Apostle himself. Thus, in John 1:6-8 we read: "6 There was a man sent from God, whose name was John (the Baptist). 7 The same came for a witness, to bear witness of the Light (jyothi-in reference to Jesus), that all men through him might believe. 8 He himself (John the Baptist himself) was not that light (jyothi) but was sent to bear witness of that light (Jesus)." John the Apostle continues and emphasizes that Jesus was the true light in John 1:9, "9 That was the true light (jyothi), which lights every man that comes into the world". We see John (the Apostle) refer to Jesus as the light several times in his Gospel. In John 3:19 he again says "19 This is the verdict: Light (Jyothi) has come into the world (referring to Jesus), but people loved darkness (thamas) instead of light (jyothi = Jesus) because their deeds were evil."

Luke, the writer of the Book of Acts in the New Testament, corroborates John (the Apostle) when he (Luke) quotes Apostle Paul, while a prisoner of Rome, as he explains to King Agrippa, the circumstances of his conversion to a follower of Jesus, because prior to his conversion, he was an ardent Jew who breathed death and destruction on the followers of Jesus.

In this account, he tells the King about his fierce opposition to the Jews who followed Jesus and an apparition he had of Jesus on his way to Damascus to persecute Jesus' disciples and to put an end to their way. During this encounter he (Paul, who then was of the name Saul) had with Jesus as narrated by Luke in Acts 26:18, we get further confirmation that Jesus is the light to turn men from darkness to light. Here, Luke quotes the conversation that Jesus had with Saul, who after this experience was baptized and became Paul the Apostle, the last (twelfth), but nonetheless no less avid a follower of Jesus and by far the most prolific in his writings. In his vision, Jesus speaks to Paul thus: "18 to open their eyes, and to turn them from darkness (thamas) to light (jyothy), and from the power of Satan (sin = thamas) unto God (purity = light), that they may receive forgiveness of sins, and inheritance among them which are sanctified by faith (in Jesus)

Image 3, Saul's Vision at Damascus Gate

As he neared Damascus on his journey, suddenly a light from heaven flashed around him. He fell to the ground and heard a voice say to him, "Saul, Saul, why do you persecute me?" "Who are you, Lord?" Saul asked. "I am Jesus, whom you are persecuting," He replied. Acts 9:3-5.

that is in me (Paul)". By the time of this conversation with the king, he (Saul) was already Paul the Apostle. The story of Paul, by the way, is one of the most powerful examples of the conversion of a ferocious opponent of Jesus, to one of his most loyal and staunch defenders, who voluntarily accepted martyrdom at the end by being crucified upside-down at his request, by the hands of the Romans, because he did not believe that he was worthy to be crucified upside-up, as his Master (Jesus) was.

Jesus is the one who came to this world to remove the darkness, the sins, from our hearts, as the prophets of old have foretold and he (Jesus) himself has testified in John 9:5, that "While I am in the world, I am the light (jyothi) of the world". It is notable that he uttered these words just before he restored the sight of a blind man, thus physically removing the darkness he lived with from his birth. His beloved disciple John also testified to Jesus being the light in 1 John 1:5, "5 This is the message we have heard from him and declare to you: God is light (jyothi); in him there is no darkness (thamas) at all".

Yes, by the fulfillment of Isaiah's prophesy in Jesus's birth, by the words of Zechariah the father of John the Baptist, the words of Simeon the old man in the temple at the time of Jesus' consecration, the words of John the Baptist, the prophet who came to prepare Jesus' way and baptized him, by Jesus' own words and the words of his Apostles, Jesus is the answer to the ancient Indian prayer "Thamaso ma Jyothirgamaya" (From darkness, lead me to light). He is the one sent for that purpose into the world and is the only one that can remove the darkness from this world. He is the Son of God who dwelt among us as man and by whom we received the fulfillment of the prayer (Shanthi Manthra) of the Upanishads to Aum, to remove the darkness (sin) that has existed in the world from the time of Adam's disobedience.

CHAPTER 4
Mruthyor Ma Amrutham Gamaya
(From Death, Lead Me to Immortality)

Of the billions of men and women who had lived on this earth, all have died or will die. It is as certain as night and day. Despite that common knowledge, at the mere mention of death, mortals tremble! Death has struck terror in the hearts of mankind ever since its entry into the world. How did death (mruthyu) enter the world? According to the Bible, the moment Eve and Adam disobeyed God, they sinned against God. That was the moment of death's birth into the world. Only two people have escaped its clutches in the natural course of life and death and they were the prophets Enoch and Elijah. In Genesis 5:24, we read, "24 Enoch walked faithfully with God; then he was no more, because God took him away." In the Book of 2 Kings 2:11 we read that as Elisha, his disciple watched, "Suddenly, a chariot of fire and horses of fire appeared and Elijah was lifted up in a whirlwind." Elisha then walked away with a tunic that fell from his master, Elijah, as he was being taken by the whirlwind.

Well aware of the mortality of man, the Saptharshies naturally yearned for immortality as much as they sought the truth as we see in their longing for it in the very first line (see chapter 5) of the manthra we are studying. In John 10:10 we read: "10 The thief comes only to steal and kill and destroy; I have come that they may have life, and have it to the full." Those are the words of Jesus who is revealing the purpose of his coming to the earth which was to give the life, which we all lost because of Adam's sin. In this chapter we will look at the Biblical evidence that he is the provider of "life" that the wise men of ancient India were seeking.

According to the Bible, death entered the world with the sins of Eve and Adam, because the punishment for sin is death as recorded in Romans 6:23, where we read that "For the wages of sin is death (mruthyu), but the gift of God is eternal life (amrutham) in Christ Jesus our Lord". The first part of the verse gives us indirect proof of the link between Adam's sin and death, because it refers to the wages of (Adam's) sin, and we can surmise that Adam's sin brought death into the world. The Scripture also gives us a direct link for Adam's sin to death in Romans 5:12; "12 Therefore, just as sin entered the world through one man (Adam), and death through sin, and in this way death came to all people, because all sinned". This verse also provides us the answer to why all men received death by Adam's sin. Death did not end with Adam, but spread to all men, and all people became sinners. Thus, all became susceptible to death because of one man's (Adam's) sin. In Romans 3:23-25, we read, "23 for all have sinned and fell short of the glory of God, 24 being justified as a gift by his grace through the redemption which is in Christ Jesus; 25 whom God displayed publicly as a propitiation in his blood through faith….". Thus death to which the entire human race was condemned to, by Adam's sin, was replaced with life by the redemption we received through the shedding of the blood of Jesus Christ at

Calvary, the mount on which Jesus was crucified. The same message is conveyed in Hebrews 13:12, "12 And so Jesus also suffered outside the city gate to make the people holy through his own blood".

Ever since Adam sinned (note that although Eve sinned first, the name always mentioned in reference to the original sin is that of Adam, because, being made from Adam's own rib, she was his own flesh and blood) and death entered the world, God in his abundant mercy had a plan for man's redemption. And that plan was the death (mruthyu) of his only Son. So, Jesus who was born "God" in the beginning of time "*without a woman*", was born "*without a man*" to a woman at the appointed time, over 2,000 years ago. He was sent to this world, for the sole purpose of the propitiation of Adam's sin and to secure eternal life for all men.

The proof is in Romans 5:17-19, "17 For if by the transgression of the one, death (mruthyu) reigned through the one (Adam), much more those who receive the abundance of grace and of the gift of righteousness will reign in life (amrutham) through the one man, Jesus Christ. 18 So then as through one transgression there resulted condemnation (death = mruthyu) to all men, even so through one act of righteousness there resulted justification of life (amrutham) to all men. 19 For as through one man's (Adam's) disobedience the many were made sinners, even so through the obedience of the one (Jesus) many will be made righteous." This is what Jesus came to accomplish. This was God's plan for man's salvation, his plan for the propitiation of the sin (disobedience) of the *first Adam* by sending his only Son, Jesus (the *second Adam*), as we read in John 3:16, "For God so loved the world that he gave his one and only Son, that whoever believes in him shall not perish (lose life or receive death = mruthyu) but have everlasting life (amrutham).

Image 4, Jesus On the Cross

After this, Jesus, knowing that all things were now accomplished, that the Scripture might be fulfilled, said, "I thirst!" Now a vessel full of sour wine was sitting there; and they filled a sponge with sour wine, put it on hyssop, and put it to His mouth. So when Jesus had received the sour wine, He said, "It is finished!" And bowing His head, He gave up His spirit. John 19:28-30.

In Ephesians 2:4, 5, Apostle Paul tells us that Jesus saved us from our transgressions which brought us death or (mruthyu) by his (Jesus') obedience. In those verses we read "4 But because of his great love for us, God (the Father), who is rich in mercy, 5 made us alive (gave us life or amrutham) with Christ even when we were dead in transgressions - it is by grace you have been saved." Again in Romans 5:10, Paul tells us that we received reconciliation and thereby redemption from death (amrutham) with "God" through Jesus' death (mruthyu); "10 For if, while we were God's enemies, we were reconciled to him (Father God) through the death (mruthyu) of his Son (Jesus), how much more, having been reconciled, shall we be saved (brought to life or to amrutham) through his (Jesus') life!". Jesus is the source of life (amrutham), and he purchased it by his death (mruthyu), for all mankind. Thus, Jesus became the ransom for the sin of Adam!

Yes, through his love, he saved us. "Greater love has no one than this" Jesus told us in John 15:13, "than to lay down his life for a friend" and he did so at the cross, and by his death (mruthyu) bought life (amrutham) to Jews and gentiles alike from his Father. Even before you and I loved him as we see in 1 John 4:19 "19We love because he first loved us", he (Jesus) loved us to the bitter end (ie. his mruthyu) as we read in John 13:1; "1It was just before the Passover Festival. Jesus knew that the hour had come for him to leave this world and go to the Father. Having loved his own who were in the world, he loved them to the end". Because of what Christ has done, we can say as we read in 1 Corinthians 15:55-57, "55 O death (mruthyu), where is thy sting? O grave, where is thy victory? 56 The sting of death is sin; and the strength of sin is the law. 57 But thanks be to God, which gives us the victory (victory over death = life = amrutham), through our Lord Jesus Christ." Yes, Jesus is the source of life (amrutham) to all mankind.

Finally, in the midst of Christ's agony before his death on the cross, as he struggled for his breath, he said two things: 1) "Father, forgive them", demonstrating his enormous patience towards his persecutors, and 2) "It is finished", before he bowed his head and died, demonstrating that he remained obedient until his death (mruthyu) on the cross to pay for the disobedience of Adam and purchase life (amrutham) for us. At this time, the curtain in the temple of Jerusalem ripped through its middle, the sun hid its face in mid-day, the earth convulsed and the doors of the sepulchers flung open giving up their dead, conquering the death (mruthyu) of many more who were already in their graves, giving them life (amrutham). The Roman soldiers trembled at the sight and their centurion seeing the manner of his death, said "Truly this man was the Son of God" as we read in Mark 15:39 and Matthew 27:54. And as Jesus hung between heaven and earth, time itself was divided into two, the one before him (BC) and the one after him, anno domini (AD), which in Latin means the year of our Lord. Yes, he divides time itself into two, the one of our bondage to sin (thamas) before his birth and the one of freedom from our bondage to sin and life (amrutham) after his death.

CHAPTER 5
Asatho Mā Sadgamaya
(From Ignorance, Lead Me to Truth)

This is the first of the four lines of the shanthi manthra we are studying. This is where the shloka starts, with a search for the truth, truth about everything, about suras (gods) of which there were many that the legends touted and the puranas detailed, truth about asuras (earthlings) and truth about life itself. The maharshies (maha-rishies) must have been somewhat baffled about the sheer number of gods. Perhaps that is why they made their supplication to Aum (the supreme god). It probably was not the only item they were puzzled about. What about the lies, the deceptions and manipulative tactics practiced by the millions of earthlings that they witnessed around them. Where is the goodness in man; they must have wondered! What about the many gods themselves choosing to employ such tactics in dealing with the asuras, they must have pondered! Yes, these probably formed only a fraction of what tormented those great minds that created the shanthi manthra. No wonder, they started the prayer with a supplication for truth. In this chapter we will examine the Biblical evidence for Jesus being the answer to that first line (first prayer) of the manthra.

Jesus is the embodiment of truth, the truth that came to us to remove the untruth that led man to sin and brought death on mankind. He is the Word that became flesh to carry out God's plan for man's salvation. That is what we learn from John 1:14, which reads, "The Word became flesh and made his dwelling among us. We have seen his glory, the glory of the one and only Son, who came from the Father, full of grace and truth (sathya)." In John 8:31–32, we read "31 To the Jews who had believed him, Jesus said, "If you hold to my teaching, you are really my disciples. 32 Then you will know the truth (sathya), and the truth will set you free (from asathya)". Jesus is the truth that came from the father to bring us the truth that will set us free from all the lies of Satan. Further in James 1:18 we read "By his own will he brought us into being, through the word of truth (sathya), so that we should have first place among all his creatures". On the night before his crucifixion, Jesus had his Last Supper with his disciples after which he gave his farewell message to them before going over to the Garden of Gethsemane where he was arrested by the Roman soldiers, and later had his trials, conviction and crucifixion. During this final sermon to his eleven disciples (Judas had already left by then to betray him), Jesus himself told his disciples about two aspects of his true being, namely truth and life, as recorded in John 14:6, "I am the way, the truth (sathya), and the life (amrutham); no one goes to the Father except by me", in one eye-opening statement.

The Gospel of John again records a conversation Jesus had with Pilate who became the prefect (governor) of the Roman province of Judea in AD 26 and was reluctant to convict Jesus of the crimes the Jewish elites accused him of, and famously washed his hands, before handing him over to the unrelenting crowd demanding his death, outside his court, in John 18:37 and 38 in which we read, "37 'You are a king, then!' said Pilate. Jesus answered, 'You say that I am a king. In fact, the reason I was born and came into the world is to testify to the truth (sathya). Everyone on the side of truth listens to me'. 38 'What is truth?' retorted Pilate. With this he went out again to the Jews who were gathered there and said, 'I find no basis for a charge against him.'" Here in this passage we see Jesus tell Pilate and re-affirm the purpose of his coming to this world, which was to bring truth (sathya) to this world.

But not everyone was willing to take Jesus at his word, nor accept him as the Messiah. In the Gospel of Matthew, we see that the Pharisees (with clandestine motives) sent their disciples to him to "trap him in his own words" and to eventually create a case against him. Thus in Matthew 22:16 we read, "And they (the Pharisees) sent their disciples to him (Jesus), along with the Herodians, saying, Teacher, we know that you are true (the embodiment of truth = sathya) and teach the way of God truthfully, and you do not care about anyone's opinion, for you are not swayed by appearances", which tells us that even those elders of the Jews who were skeptical about Jesus' authenticity as the Son of God, did experience that he (Jesus) was known for being truth (sathya) itself, as stated by him and believed by his disciples. One may say that the disciples of the Pharisees and the Herodians did not mean what they said, and sure enough it may be so, because they were trying to trap him in His words and make him commit a crime against Rome!

Their question to him was whether it was, as we read in Matthew 22:17, "Tell us then, what is your opinion? Is it right to pay the imperial tax to Caesar or not?" Pharisees and the Herodians who at that time were plotting to kill him, calculated that if Jesus said "Yes" He would alienate the Jews who were adamantly opposed to the Roman's interfering in their right for self-government and if he said "No", they could make a case against him for defying Rome whose officers at that time were extremely alert to any sign of resistance to Rome from any one and would prosecute them. The trap they set was perfect in their mind. So, let us move on to examine his answer.

In a stunning demonstration of his insight into the treachery behind their question and their evil design, Jesus asked them to bring him a coin, which they did. Jesus asked them whose name and emblem were on it and they correctly answered that it was Caesar's as we read in Matthew 22:18-21. "18 But Jesus, knowing their evil intent, said, 'You hypocrites, why are you trying to trap me? 19 Show me the coin used for paying the tax.' They brought him a denarius, 20 and he asked them, 'Whose image is this? And whose inscription?' 21 'Caesar's,' they replied. Then he said to them, 'So give back to Caesar what is Caesar's, and to God what is God's.'" The men were dumbfounded at his wisdom and logic and simply walked away, demonstrating that he was "true and taught the way of God truthfully, did not care about anyone's opinion, and that he was not swayed by appearances", just as they said to him, whether or not they meant it!

Impecunious as he was, Jesus paid his taxes. Elsewhere (Matthew 17:27) we read that Jesus once asked Peter, his disciple to go fish and instructed him to take a four-drachma coin he would find in the fish's mouth and to pay the taxes for Peter and Jesus himself, "that they may not cause offense". Jesus was not just talk. He walked his talk! He too "Paid unto Caesar, what was due unto Caesar!"

Image 5, Peter Finding Coin in A Fish's Mouth to Pay Taxes

But so that we may not cause offense, go to the lake and throw out your line. Take the first fish you catch; open its mouth and you will find a four-drachma coin. Take it and give it to them for my tax and yours." Matthew 17:27.

Surely he was truth itself in flesh as was stated above in John 1:14. Three verses later, in his Gospel (John 1:17), we read, "For the law was given through Moses; grace and truth (sathya) came through Jesus Christ." Again in the First Book of John, (1 John 2:8) we read that "8 Yet I am writing you a new command; its truth (sathya) is seen in him (Jesus) and in you, because the darkness (thamas) is passing and the true light (jyothi) is already shining", confirming that Jesus is the truth, that came as truth itself to bring us light that removes darkness from this world.

CHAPTER 6
Oṁ Śhānti Śhānti Śhāntiḥ
(Ohm Peace, Peace, Peace!)

This is the fourth and final verse of the incantation as it is commonly chanted. The word peace is recited three times here and according to different scholars, each iteration of the word "peace" represents a different invocation for peace. Accordingly, it represents removing physical, divine and internal obstacles. It is also said to symbolize three forms of peace, ie., of the mind, of speech and of the body. Others believe that the three iterations of shanthi represent individual, collective and universal peace. Regardless of the various interpretations, one thing is certain that the writers of the Shanthi Manthra were a race that craved for universal peace.

In this chapter we will examine the Biblical evidence that Jesus is the fulfillment of the chant for peace in the Shanthi Manthra which is the subject of this book and that he is the prince of peace to come to earth as predicted by the prophet Isaiah, proclaimed by the angels to the shepherds on the first Christmas day, brought peace to Simeon who had the promise of God that he will not die before he sees the one who is to deliver the people of Israel on the day of Jesus's dedication in the Temple of Jerusalem, and then left His peace on earth with his disciples to pass it on to all, before he ascended back into the heavens to return to his Father.

Before I undertake the task of proving that Jesus is the "prince of peace" to come as prophesied by Isaiah, let us examine the veracity of the Book of Isaiah itself, because skeptics have long claimed that it was written after the birth of Jesus, thus nullifying its prophetic validity. The prophet Isaiah lived during the reigns of Uzziah, Jotham, Ahaz, and Hezekiah (742-687 BC) of Judah, the southern Kingdom of Israel. The proof that his Book in the Bible and his writings were authentic came in 1947 with the discovery of the Dead Sea Scrolls, a set of scrolls written on parchment and hidden in caves by members of a monastic religious sect of Judaism known as the Essenes that emerged near Qumran, near the Dead Sea, about 200 BC. They diligently observed the edicts of their religion and eagerly waited for the Messiah (the redeemer) of Israel. John the Baptist is believed to have belonged to this sect. The collection of writings included an intact scroll of the Book of Isaiah thereby verifying that the prophecies of Isaiah about Jesus were genuine and were written before their fulfillment. By all we know and by the best evidence we have about the time the Upanishads were written, Isaiah was a contemporary of its writers. His writings were influenced by the moral breakdown of the times and his yearning for his people to return to their God Jehovah. It was a sentiment he must have shared with the writers of the Upanishads who also craved for truth, life, light and peace in their land, and who by inference must have been similarly troubled by their people living in the darkness of sin and dying with no one to give them the light to show them the truth they needed to turn away from their evil ways and receive peace.

Isaiah reminded his countrymen of the need to keep God's covenant if the Israelites were to remain God's chosen people. He hoped for and predicted a redeemer to come for their salvation. In that vein, the Book contains two of the most famous prophecies in Hebrew Scripture; those of (1) the Virgin birth of the Messiah (Isaiah 7:14) and (2) the birth of the Messiah described as a servant who would suffer and die for our sins (Isaiah 52:13 – 53:12), and who was later identified and reaffirmed as Jesus Christ in the New Testament. The first about the birth of Jesus in Isaiah 7:14 reads as follows; "14 Therefore the Lord himself will give you a sign: The virgin will conceive and give birth to a son, and will call him Immanuel (God with us)." The materialization of this prophesy is described in Matthew 1:18-25 and Luke 1:26-38. The fulfillment of the second one about his suffering (the Passion of Christ) prophesied in Isaiah 52 and 53 is depicted in Luke 24:26 and 24:46. We see the fulfillment of this in the story as told by Luke in chapter 24 about a man by the name of Cleopas who was travelling from Jerusalem to Emmaus with another disciple and were talking about the brutal persecution and the heinous death that Jesus their Master had to go through on the cross. Jesus, whom they did not recognize then as him at first, walked by them and reminded them that the manner of his death was no accident, but was preplanned by Father God himself by quoting the scriptures from Moses through all the prophets. As he concludes his lesson in prophesies to the two men, he asks them as stated in Luke 24:26, "Did not the Messiah have to suffer these things and then enter his glory?" and in 24:46 he points out that, "This is what is written: The Messiah will suffer and rise from the dead on the third day" according to the prophesies. Cleopas and his friend recognized who it was that explained these things to them only when they persuaded him to stay with them overnight and they broke bread together, later that evening.

It is Isaiah who prophesied the coming of Jesus as the light (jyothi) that will remove the darkness (thamas) from among his people in Isaiah 9:6 in which we read "For unto us a child is born, unto us a son is given: and the government shall be upon his shoulder: and his name shall be called Wonderful, Counselor, The mighty God, The everlasting Father, The Prince of Peace (shanthi)". Here among other things, Isaiah refers to Jesus as the Prince of Peace (shanthi), a sentiment echoed again in the announcement of Jesus' birth by the angels to the shepherds who were diligently watching their flock at night on the night of his birth and were the first ones to be notified of Jesus's birth in a lowly manger in Bethlehem, because his parents could not find a place for the night of his birth at the local inn, during their sojourn to their ancestral land as ordered by Caesar Augustus for a census he decreed, again to fulfill the prophesy about the place of his birth.

This fact is recorded in the Gospel of Luke 2:8-14. "8 And there were shepherds living out in the fields nearby, keeping watch over their flocks at night. 9 An angel of the Lord appeared to them, and the glory of the Lord shone around them, and they were terrified. 10 But the angel said to them, "Do not be afraid. I bring you good news that will cause great joy for all the people. 11 Today in the town of David a Savior has been born to you; he is the Messiah, the Lord. 12 This will be a sign to you: You will find a baby wrapped in cloths and lying in a manger." 13 Suddenly a great company of the heavenly host appeared with the angel, praising God and saying, 14 "Glory to God in the highest heaven, and on earth peace (shanthi) to those on whom his favor rests." This was an affirmation of Isaiah's prophesy of the birth of a baby (Jesus) who would be a prince, a prince of peace. Notice that in verse 10, the angels proclaimed peace not only for the shepherds, but for all the people. It is qualified in verse 14 with the proviso "on whom his favor rests", implying as elsewhere stated that, that peace is available to everyone who believes in him, because we have his promise that "his favor will rest" on those who believe in him.

We have already seen in the section on "Thamaso Ma Jyothirgamaya", (Chapter 3) how Zechariah the priest and the father of John the Baptist was filled with the Holy Ghost (Luke 1:67) when he saw his newborn baby (John) who was to become John the Baptist in due course and prophesied that John will be a prophet and be the forerunner of Jesus as narrated in Luke 1:76-79. In verse 76 Zechariah prophesies that his son will be a prophet, the "Prophet of the Most High" who is to point the way to the "dayspring from on high" (Jesus) mentioned in verse 78. That there will be one clearing the way for Jesus too was prophesied by Isaiah, in Isaiah 40:3 which reads, "A voice is calling, 'Clear the way for the Lord in the wilderness; make smooth in the desert a highway for our God." The fact that a prophet (John the Baptist) was to come before Jesus as his forerunner was also foretold by the prophet Malachi in Malachi 3:1 in which we read "Behold, I am going to send My messenger, and he will clear the way before Me. And the Lord whom you seek, will suddenly come to His temple; and the messenger of the covenant, in whom you delight, behold, He is coming," says the Lord of hosts." Luke 1:76 and 77, as spoken by Zechariah, is again in reference to John the Baptist, who was to come before Jesus (Luke 1:78) who was born to bring "light (jyothi) to those who lived in darkness (thamas) and in the shadow of death (mruthyu) and lastly to guide their feet into the way of peace (shanthi).

We also saw another scene earlier in this discourse about an elderly man in the temple of Jerusalem where Jesus was brought for his consecration. That man was Simeon mentioned in Luke 2:29-32, wherein he receives peace (shanthi) as he saw Jesus and obtained the fulfillment of God's promise to him that he will not see death until he sees God's promised Messiah. At the sight of Jesus, he was moved by the Spirit and said "Sovereign Lord, as you have promised, you may now dismiss your servant in peace (shanthi). For my eyes have seen your salvation, which you have prepared in the sight of all nations: a light (jyothi) for revelation to the Gentiles, and the glory of your people Israel". Simeon too was filled with peace (shanthi) as he saw baby Jesus, long before Jesus' public ministry on earth began, 31 years later.

Image 6, Simeon Receiving Peace at the Sight of Infant Jesus

As soon as Simeon beheld baby Jesus, he was miraculously moved by the Spirit and said this: "Sovereign Lord, as you have promised, you may now dismiss your servant in peace. For my eyes have seen your salvation (the Messiah), which you have prepared in the sight of all nations: a light for revelation to the Gentiles, and the glory of your people Israel". Luke 2:29-32.

Finally, Jesus left his peace with us as he left his earthly body. In his speech to his disciples during the time of his Last supper, he consoles his disciples in John 14:27 by saying, "Peace (shanthi) I leave with you; my peace (shanthi) I give to you. Not as the world gives do I give to you. Let not your hearts be troubled, neither let them be afraid." When he said this, Jesus was well aware of the fact that his earthly journey as a man was about to end and of the tumult that his departure would create in the lives of his chosen disciples. Therefore He spent the whole evening consoling them and assuring them that his peace (shanthi) will be with them before he was to face his death.

Towards the end of his message to them, again in John 16:33 we read, "33 I have told you these things, so that in me you may have peace (shanthi). In this world you will have trouble. But take heart! I have overcome the world". Jesus thus solidifies their faith in him at that juncture, as his own death was looming and the disciples' loss was impending. Jesus was well aware also of the persecution his disciples were to face in the very near future and again is making it a point to firm up their faith by telling them that he is well aware of what awaits them and points out to them that he is no stranger to such afflictions and that with faith in him, they too can overcome the world. He reassured them in that speech that he will leave his peace (shanthi) that he was able to bring to their lives during their short (earthly) life with him, just as he calmed the storm for them in the Sea of Galilee and brought peace (shanthi) to them in their time of anxiety as the storm tossed their boat in the Sea of Galilee on that fateful day while Jesus slept in peace in the very same boat. What foresight, what kindness and what empathy he was able to show his disciples as he knew what horror he himself was going to go through in the coming hours of his own life!

CHAPTER 7

Jesus the Fulfillment of the Shanthi Manthra

In John 3:19 Jesus tells Nicodemus, "This is the verdict: Light (jyothi) has come into the world, but people loved darkness instead of light because their deeds were evil." He gave his life for us as Isaiah foresaw and foretold in Isaiah 53:5 "But he was pierced for our transgressions, he was crushed for our iniquities; the punishment that brought us peace (shanthi) was on him, and by his wounds we are healed."

Yes, he was wounded and accepted death (mruthyu) according to his Father's plan and by it brought us peace (shanthi). Yes, Jesus was the fulfillment of Isaiah's prophesy of a prince of peace to come, and today, he remains the source of peace to the entire humanity. His peace he did leave with us as we can see the way his disciples, most of them humble fishermen, suffered persecution at the hands of the powerful Roman Government, yet peacefully prevailed and told their story for which they were eyewitnesses so that to this day we can retell that story to the world, thanks to their conviction and courage. Because of their sacrifice, we too can enjoy that peace. He made it our mandate to pass it on to posterity.

Jesus was life and light at the same time as we read in John 1:4; "4 In him was life (amrutham), and that life was the light (jyothi)" of all mankind. In John 1:10-13 we read "10 He was in the world, and though the world was made through him, the world did not recognize him. 11 He came to that which was his own, but his own (the Jews) did not receive him. 12 Yet to all who did receive him (Jew or Gentile), to those who believed in his name, he gave the right to become children of God - 13 children born not of natural descent, nor of human decision or a husband's will, but born of God."

The world could not tolerate him (the light) and they crucified him, but death (mruthyu) could not conquer him. According to Peter, his disciple, as we read in Acts 2:24 "24 But God raised him from the dead, freeing him from the agony of death, because it was impossible for death to keep its hold on him." His sepulcher could not contain him. Up from the grave he arose and mightily triumphed over his foes. He arose a victor from the dark domain and lives with his father to return to gather his saints and to fetter the Satan forever at the end of time. Thereafter, he will reign supreme in the heavens with the redeemed in Christ. He arose; He arose. Hallelujah, Christ Arose! He says "I am the living One; I was dead, and now look, I am alive for ever and ever! And I hold the keys of hell and death, (Rev 1:18). He arose and gave us his promise, before he finished his terrestrial existence in flesh and ascended into the skies, that he will dwell in all those who would believe in him.

There is only one name that fits the description of being light, life and truth all in one, and has brought peace to humanity. He has already delivered this humanly impossible, this lofty, this supernal objective of removing the darkness, untruth and death from humanity and bringing eternal peace to those who would diligently seek him and simply accept him as their savior!

In Ephesians 5:13, 14, we read that, "13 But everything exposed by the light (jyothi) becomes visible - and everything that is illuminated becomes a light. 14 This is why it is said: 'Wake up, sleeper, rise from the dead, and Christ will shine on you.'" In Luke 1:78, 79 we read that "Because of the tender mercy of our God, with which the Sunrise from on high (the light that is Jesus Christ) will visit us". Yes, he visited us and those who have received that light by believing in him have become that light for him in this world. In Ephesians 5:8-11 we read that, "8 For you were once darkness (thamas), but now you are light (jyothi) in the Lord. Live as children of light (jyothi) 9 (for the fruit of the light consists in all goodness, righteousness and truth) 10 and find out what pleases the Lord. 11 Have nothing to do with the fruitless deeds of darkness (thamas), but rather expose them." Yes, we were once darkness, but those who have woken up from their slumber and have received the light are lights themselves according to Matthew 5:14-16 which reads "14 You are the light (jyothi) of the world. A town built on a hill cannot be hidden. 15 Neither do people light a lamp and put it under a bowl. Instead they put it on its stand, and it gives light (jyothi) to everyone in the house. 16 In the same way, let your light (jyothi) shine before others, that they may see your good deeds and glorify your Father in heaven." That is the calling for Christians. <u>Christians are lighted by Christ to lighten others.</u> That is why they reflect the light they themselves received, on to others. That is their mandate and their mission!

Image 7, Lighted to Lighten

See to it, then, that the light within you is not darkness. Therefore, if your whole body is full of light, and no part of it dark, it will be just as full of light as when a lamp shines its light on you." Luke 11:35, 36.

He is the fulfillment of the Shanthi Manthra. He is Jesus Christ, our Master and our Lord. He is light (jyothi), he is truth (sathya), he is life (amrutham) and he is the prince of peace (shanthi). He is the one who brought all three of the exhortations in the Shanthi Manthra to remove thamas, asathya and mruthyu to fruition and materialized the manthra's invocation for peace (shanthi) on earth, not only for the Jews but for the entire humanity, as we see in Revelations 5:9. "And they sang a new song, saying: 'You are worthy to take the scroll and to open its seals, because you were slain, and with your blood you purchased for God, persons from every tribe and language and people and nation."

Yes, as it was declared by Peter the Apostle, the cornerstone of the Christian faith, in 1 Peter 2:9, where we read "But you are a chosen people, a royal priesthood, a holy nation, God's special possession, that you may declare the praises of him who called you out of darkness (thamas) into his wonderful light (jyothi). Paul, Christ's Apostle, also has said "For God . . . made his light shine in our hearts to give us the light (jyothi) of the knowledge of God's glory light, of the knowledge of God's glory displayed in the face of Christ", in 2 Corinthians 4:6. Yes, Christians have received the grace because he (Jesus) came and dwelled among us as is said in John 1:14. So Christians cannot hide the truth. Christians do not put that light they received under the bushel, they shine it from the hills, because even in death, they will live in Christ as we read about it, in his discourse with Martha, before he was about to raise Lazarus from the dead in John 11:25, 26, "25 Jesus said to her, "I am the resurrection and the life (amrutham). The one who believes in me will live, even though they die (succumb to mruthyu); 26 and whoever lives by believing in me will never die. Do you believe this?" The words Jim Elliott, the 20th Century Martyr for Christ among the people of the Huaorani tribe in Equador "He is no fool who gives what he cannot keep to gain that which he cannot lose" are poignant here and speaks for the countless martyrs for Christ since the first Century. Christians are "a people" who have given their lives (which no one can keep forever) to Christ to receive eternal life, amrutham, (which no one can take away from them); through their belief in Christ. No persecution and no power on earth can put out that light that will shine in their lives forevermore, once it dwells in them.

CHAPTER 8

A Message to the People of India

Let us wake up. Let us open our eyes and see the irony. The Christians who are trying to show the one (the _Aum_, the real Aum) by whom the prayers of the sages of ancient India and the countless pious Hindus of posterity since, thus making him no longer "a mystery" but forever _"known"_, are the ones that are being persecuted the most, around the world. According to the International Society of Human Rights, a secular group with 38 member states in the world, 80% of religious discrimination in the world in 2017, was against Christians and according to the Center for the Study of Global Christianity, many Christians die every year because of their faith. India is not to be blamed for all this, but India, the land of peace and tolerance, the land of the Saptharshies does not have to be sharing in this staggering and unjust statistic.

So, wake up, land of the munies (sages), wakeup land of the rishies (saints), wake up land of shanthi (peace). Open your eyes Bhāratha Mātha (Mother India), and see the paradox. The very people who are suffering persecution at the hands of the religious fanatics, the likes of Nathuram Godse, today, are the ones who are simply trying to show everyone, the "light" that came to this world (Jesus), and who actually delivered on the prayer, the incantation, the Shanthi Manthra of the maharishies of ancient India. Listen to what was said in John 1:9, he is "The true light that gives light (jyothi) to everyone….in the world." Speak up now, or there will be none left later to speak for anyone, except the stones and the dust.

That savior is none other than the son of David, he is none other than the Lion of Judah, he is the Word, the Word that became flesh, he is the Son of God, who became a son of man. He is the Lamb of God. As was prophesied by Isaiah he is the lamb that remained silent before his persecutors as is written in Isaiah 53:7, in which we read, "He was oppressed and afflicted, yet he did not open his mouth; he was led like a lamb to the slaughter, and as a sheep before its shearers is silent, so he did not open his mouth." He is the Lamb of God that was slaughtered once and for all and replaced the slaughter of animals forever as sacrifices for our sins.

Let me alert all those who are persecuting the Christians for showing the light they received, to others, wherever they are, the experience of Saul (later Paul the Apostle) as he approached the gate of Damascus as we read in Acts 9:3-6, "3 As he neared Damascus on his journey, suddenly a light from heaven flashed around him. 4 He fell to the ground and heard a voice say to him, "Saul, Saul, why do you persecute me?" and the admonition Paul recounts in front of King Agrippa, in Acts 26:14, "It is hard for you to kick against the pricks", an analogy used in that verse of the image of a bull or a beast of burden fruitlessly kicking against the goad of its owner or the horse against the spur of its equestrian master. Christ's intervention in his life made Saul (a Roman by birth, a Pharisee by ancestry and a fierce warrior by his faith against Christendom in its infancy; one of Christ's most powerful witnesses as he became Paul the Apostle, who in all his persecution about which he boasts in 2 Corinthians 11:23-27), the prime example of perseverance in persecution in the name of the one he himself persecuted before his conversion, even to this day!

This Jesus has been painted before our very eyes from the time of Isaiah, the same time the sages that created the Upanishad's scribed the Shanti Manthra and began the chant. Let the Christians shine his light of truth and give people life through that truth. Let us wake up, my fellow Indians. Let us return the right of the people of India, their freedom of thought and choice of the spiritual life they yearn, whatsoever it may be, which is guaranteed to them in their constitution, envisioned by Bappuji and his followers, by removing the barriers to such freedom of thought and choice. We owe it to the ancient sages of India to bring peace to the country. When that happens, all those who choose to believe in Jesus Christ, will be justified and will have eternal life (amrutham) and peace (shanthi), a peace offered by Jesus in our hearts as we learn from Romans 5:1, "Therefore, since we have been justified through faith, we have peace (shanthi) with God through our Lord Jesus Christ". Our Bhāratha Mātha will be so much the better for it! We owe it to Mahatma Gandhi and his followers who worked tirelessly to create a secular India by incorporating religious tolerance in our constitution. To all those who are determined to persist in the path of persecution of Christians, let me paraphase the words of Jesus at the gate of Damascus to Saul, "It is hard for one to kick against the pricks!"

POSTSCRIPT
Mea Culpa

Any Roman Catholic individual who reads this book will understand the meaning of the Latin phrase meā culpā. Those who do not know what it means, will understand it as you read on. The Bible says in Romans 3:23, that, "23 for all have sinned and fall(en) short of the glory of God," indicating our sinful nature. But this is not the idea that I intend to convey with the use of the phrase "mea culpa" here, because in the next verse, it tells us about the redemption we received, "24 and all are justified freely by his grace through the redemption that came by Christ Jesus" because of Jesus' death. My use of the phrase here is to indicate the culpability of Christians for the sparsity of Christianity in India at this time, the dawn of the 21st century, even though Christianity took its root in India as early as 52 AD with the arrival of St. Thomas (The Doubting Thomas) in India, on the west coast of Kerala. Let me add that such sparsity is not entirely the fault of Christians, nor because they haven't tried.

It is believed, and there is plenty of historic evidence that Apostle Thomas arrived on the Malabar Coast in the now lost Port of Muziri (probably the Anglicized version of Muchiri) and known by several other names including Mahodayapuram, believed to be in Kodungallur, 18 miles north of Cochin, the Anglicized name of the ancient city of Kochi. After his arrival there, it is believed that he baptized four prominent Nampoothiri Families known as Pakalomattam, Kalli, Kali Kavu and Shankaram. Legend has it that he continued his journey from there through

Kerala, reaching Madura (Madras) and established "Seven and a half" churches along the way before his assassination and martyrdom because of which, he could not complete the eighth one.

Apostle Thomas is considered the Patron Saint of Christians in India. However, there is some speculation that another Apostle of Jesus, Saint Bartholomew also came to India and had a mission in the Mumbai (Bombay) region on the Konkan coast, a region which has been known for the ancient port town of Kalyan, where he was eventually martyred. Eusebius of Caesarea (early 4th century) and Saint Jerome (late 4th century), both refer to this tradition while speaking of the reported visit of Pantaenus, a Christian scholar from Alexandria, to India in the 2nd century, although there is some debate as to whether St. Jerome who wrote about this, confused Bartholomew (Bar Tolmai in Hebrew) with Mar Thoma (St. Thomas) and whether the two were referring to Arabia or Persia rather than India in their writings. The St. Thomas legend has a lot of credibility, nonetheless. In spite of this early arrival of Christianity in India, it is only the third common religion in India, and only a tiny fraction at that.

Despite the fact that Apostle Thomas arrived in India following Jesus' command as recorded by Matthew in Matthew 28:19-20, "19 Therefore go and make disciples of all nations, baptizing them in the name of the Father and of the Son and of the Holy Spirit (The Christian Trinity), 20 and teaching them to obey everything I have commanded you. And surely I am with you always, to the very end of the age" and Mark in Mark 16:15, "15 And he said unto them, Go ye into all the world, and preach the Gospel to every creature", in the first Century itself, his followers (the St. Thomas Christians), have not been able to carry on that mission to spread the Gospel of Christ to any great extent in India.

They, the St. Thomas Christians, in the early days were known as Nazaranies as they followed the "Nazarene", another name attributed to Jesus because he (Jesus) grew up in the town of Nazareth. The Nazaranies lived in harmony with the Hindus, adopting some of their cultural practices such as the "thalikettu", the practice of the groom tying the thali, (a special pendant) around the bride's neck as part of the marriage ritual during their marriage ceremonies, popularizing the term "tying the knot" to mean "marriage" in the English language. Early St. Thomas Christians were known to have kept the nilavilakku in their churches and homes. They were guests of honor and were invited by Hindus to light their lamps during their ceremonies. Margam Kali, a special dance by Christian women, was, at one time, said to take place around a nilavilakku.

Perhaps such amiability and the lack of resistance were the reasons why Christianity did not spread widely in India. Some scholars believe that no other culture or country in the world was as tolerant to any religion as the Hindus in India were to Christianity in its early days and no one gave Christians as much freedom to spread their religion as the Indians did. Yet, according to the census of 2011, there were approximately 28 million Christians in India, constituting only 2.3 percent of India's population at that time. This, after 2000 years of Christianity in India is dismal from a statistical point of view for the Christians. Why? Are Christians to be blamed for their lackluster performance in spreading the Gospel of Jesus Christ in India?

No, not at all! The Christian Missionaries did a yeoman's job of spreading the Gospel in India. They too were not any more successful than the Nazaranis in improving on the statistic. There is no definitive answer to the question of such slow growth of Christianity in India, but speculations abound. In India Christians encountered a culture that did not resist it. Neither did the Hindus embrace it wholeheartedly because they did not find it exceptional. Many Hindus took Christ as one of their many gods and added "it" to their collection of icons, rather than the sole savior of their souls. The words of the Sanskrit scholar Monier Williams are very relevant in this regard. In 1878 he wrote that "Clearly, then, the chief impediment to Christianity among Indians is not only the pride they feel in their own (Hindu) religion, but the very nature of that religion. For pantheism is a most subtle, plausible and all-embracing system, which may profess to include Christianity itself as one of the phenomena of the universe." An eminent Hindu is reported to have said: "We Hindus have no need of conversion; we are more than Christians already."

E. Stanley Jones was a famous (Methodist) missionary, who went to India in 1907 and served there through the 1950's. He was a confidant of leaders of the USA and India, who worked hard for world peace and was once nominated for the Nobel Peace Prize. He was elected a Bishop in the Methodist Church but refused to accept the office, preferring to remain a missionary, because he always considered himself an evangelist, trying to share Jesus Christ with those who did not know him. He became a close friend of Mahatma Gandhi, after he came to know him and wrote a book about Gandhi.

Stanley Jones greatly admired Mahatma Gandhi and considered Gandhiji the greatest man that he ever knew. He tried unsuccessfully to convert him into a Christian. Jones said that he learned very much from Gandhi. Perhaps we can learn some from him and his book "Mahatma Gandhi An Interpretation".

Here is an excerpt from Stanley Jones about the greatness of Gandhiji: "Take the Cross. Mahatma Gandhi did not see in the Cross, what the convinced Christian sees, namely, that God was in Christ reconciling the world unto himself and that he was bearing our sins in his body on a tree. Gandhi did not see that. But he did see that you can take on suffering yourself, and not give it, and thus conquer the heart of another. That he did see in the Cross, and that he put into practice, and put it into practice on a national scale. The difference then is this: we as Christians saw more in the Cross than Gandhi and put it into operation less; Gandhi saw less in the Cross than we and put it into practice more. We left the Cross a doctrine; Gandhi left it a deed. Therefore Gandhi, with his half-light and fuller practice, goes in power beyond us who have fuller light and half-practice. God therefore accepts his operative deed and entrusts him with power, while God can use in only a limited way our faith, which is minus the operative deed. God apparently has to pass by the orthodoxy and use the orthopraxy. Do not misunderstand me. I do not minimize right belief; it is necessary. But 'not everyone that saith unto me, Lord, Lord, shall enter into the kingdom of heaven; but he that doeth the will of my Father which is in heaven.'" The lesson: do not just preach, but practice Christianity.

It was while studying Law in England that Gandhiji became interested in Christianity. He was fascinated by the teachings of Christ, and he quoted frequently from the "Sermon on the Mount". We do not know why he did not become a Christian, but a story has been told, that once while in South Africa, he attempted to attend a worship service in a church. As he went up the steps to the door, he was approached by an elder (a greeter, perhaps who asked him, "Where he was going?" Gandhiji said that he wanted to attend the service, to which the elder allegedly replied "We have no use for fakirs in this church, please leave or I will have my assistants throw you down the steps". One has to wonder if this is why, when asked why he is not a Christian? Gandhiji's response was "I like the Christ, but not the Christians!" If true, this is an example of how a Christian is not to behave to another person. One can only imagine what an advocate Gandhiji would have been for Christianity in India, if only the elder in this story had acted with genuine Christian love toward him!

Without pointing finger at the Christians, let me state that a bit of introspection is appropriate at this point. Are we Christians truly reflecting the life of our Savior in our daily walk? It is time we Christians examine our own behavior in front of non-Christians in India. Are we emulating Christ in our dealings with others? Is our behavior one that honors Christ? Are we doing unto others as we would have them do unto us? Are we reflecting the light that we received (Christ) in our daily walk? Are we shining the light of Christ that we have been lighted with on others whom we come across? "For we are to God the pleasing aroma of Christ among those who are being saved and those who are perishing (2 Cor 2:15). Are we living up to that expectation? Are we "Making our gentleness evident to all?", as the Apostle Paul instructs us in Philippians 4:5. Or, are we the reason that Christianity did not prosper so far in India, because we did not live up to that standard? This is the time for self-examination. This is our time to become the new creatures in Christ if any of us has been short in our imitation of Christ. As Paul instructs us through his letter to the Church in Rome in Romans 13: 12: "The night is nearly over; the day is almost here. So let us put aside the deeds of darkness and put on the armor of light." Let us ask ourselves, "Do we need a little more of orthopraxy than orthodoxy, as Dr. Stanley Jones put it?"

I believe the words of Apostle Paul in Philippians 4:4-9 are worth repeating here, "4 Rejoice in the Lord always. I will say it again: Rejoice! 5 Let your gentleness be evident to all. The Lord is near. 6 Do not be anxious about anything, but in every situation, by prayer and petition, with thanksgiving, present your requests to God. 7 And the peace (shanthi) of God, which transcends all understanding, will guard your hearts and your minds in Christ Jesus. 8 Finally, brothers and sisters, whatever is true, whatever is noble, whatever is right, whatever is pure, whatever is lovely, whatever is admirable—if anything is excellent or praiseworthy—think about such things. 9 Whatever you have learned or received or heard from me, or seen in me—put it into practice. And the God of peace (shanthi) will be with you." In other words, my friends, let us cast out churchianity and embrace Christianity.

This book is my humble effort to reveal and reflect the small glimmer of light (the bodhodaya that I received while attending the reception I mentioned in the introduction), to the Nation of India, my country of origin. My fellow men and women of India, I hope that this book shall enlighten you and open your minds about the true meaning of the Shanthi Manthra that I tried to re-interpret in this monograph. I also hope that it will help my fellow Christians as a means to connect with their Hindu friends in their attempt to tell them who Christ is! If we all can do so, perhaps the new millennium can be a lot more positive for Christianity in India than the previous two.

In conclusion, this is my prayer. May the everlasting love of God our Father, the redeeming mercies of Jesus Christ our brother and the abiding presence of the Holy Ghost the counselor, be with each and every one of us, now and forevermore.

Aum, shanthi, shanthi, shanthi.

MORE ABOUT THE AUTHOR
Kalarickal Joseph Oommen, MD, FAAN, FAES, FACNS, Lubbock, Texas, USA

Dr. K. J. Oommen was born in Alleppey (Alappuzha), a coastal district of Kerala India, and grew up in Chennemkary, a small agricultural farming village known for its extensive paddy (rice) fields and coconut palms. His parents were the 11th generation of the Kallakkadampil branch of the Pakalomattam family of Nazarani Christians whose ancestors went there in the first half of the 18th century and became part of the history of Kuttanadu by participating in the conversion of the crocodile infested marshlands into paddy fields, which at one time earned the tehsil, the reputation of the "rice bowl" of Kerala. After receiving his higher secondary education with first class distinction, in a Roman Catholic (St. Mary's) high school in the nearby village of Kainakary, he received his undergraduate degree with first class distinction in Chemistry and Physics from the Sanathana Dharma College in Kalarkodu, Alappuzha. The following year, he taught Chemistry in the historic Church Mission Society (CMS) College, Kottayam, in Kerala, while preparing to enter one of the three government-run medical colleges in Kerala. After obtaining his Doctorate in Medicine with the degree of Bachelor of Medicine and Bachelor of Surgery (MBBS) form the Trivandrum (Thiruvananthapuram) Medical College, he served briefly as a medical officer in two different Christian hospitals in the next year, while preparing for the examination of the Educational Commission for Foreign Medical Graduates (ECFMG) of the United States of America (USA).

The following year, in 1975 he arrived in the USA and worked in a State Hospital in Missouri in a small town, famous for the Westminster College in Fulton, the venue of the "Iron Curtain Speech" by Winston Churchill, at a defining moment in World History, which saw the shifting away of the Western powers from an alliance with Russia towards the ideological and political state we now call the "Cold War" era. After serving in the Fulton State Hospital, for seven months, he joined a Psychiatry Residency at the University of Arizona in Tucson Arizona, where he subsequently completed a Neurology Residency as well. Next he trained in advanced Epilepsy management in the Clinical Neurophysiology Fellowship Program of the University of Georgia in Augusta, Georgia, where he served as an instructor during his fellowship and as an Assistant Professor of Neurology for a year thereafter, before moving back to Arizona and Joining the Department of Neurology of the University of Arizona as Assistant Professor of Neurology and as the Chief of Neurology at The Kino Community Hospital, an affiliate of the University Medical Center in Tucson, Arizona at that time.

During the next 10 years, he worked tirelessly in establishing The Arizona Comprehensive Epilepsy Program (ACEP), the first ever Level 4 (as defined by the National Association of Epilepsy Centers in the US) Epilepsy Center in the State, and became its Founding Medical Director, progressing at the same time to the level of Associate Clinical Professor in the Department of Neurology of the University of Arizona. He was then invited by the Department of Neurology of the University of Oklahoma to develop a Comprehensive Epilepsy Center there. After joining the faculty as an Associate Professor of Neurology, he developed the first Level 4 epilepsy center in Oklahoma City, Oklahoma.

While continuing to build the program, he rose to the rank of Professor of Neurology in the University of Oklahoma. After serving there for 14 years as the Medical Director of the Comprehensive Oklahoma Program Epilepsy (COPE), he was recruited by the Texas Tech Health Sciences Center (TTUHSC) as the First Crofoot Chair of Epilepsy in the Department of Neuropsychiatry in the Texas Tech health Sciences Center. Two years later, he moved to the Private Sector, continuing as the Co-Medical Director of the Jay and Virginia Crofoot Epilepsy Monitoring Unit (JVCEMU) at the Covenant Hospital in Lubbock, Texas, until 2019. Currently (2022) he serves as a staff physician at the Covenant Hospital and the as the Director of the Epilepsy Clinics of the Covenant Medical Group.

During this period (1982 to 2022), that covered a span of 40 years, Dr. Oommen trained hundreds of medical students, dozens of residents, and six specialists (fellows) in Clinical Neurophysiology and Epilepsy. In the same period, he served as principal investigator for over 60 industry sponsored epilepsy drug research projects, leading to the US Federal Drug Administration (FDA) approval of about a dozen new antiepileptic drugs and the Deep Brain Stimulator (DBS), an electronic device for the treatment of epilepsy and authored over 100 research abstracts and 37 peer reviewed articles. He was also active in continuing education and organized dozens of Neurology and Epilepsy grand rounds and twenty Regional Conferences in Neuroscience in the three states he worked in.

When asked what drove him to continue on the rigorous path he followed in patient care, education and research, he replied that his goal in life is to emulate Christ in the two of the most important things he did on earth during his earthly ministry, which were healing and teaching. But when asked why he had such a passion for research, which Jesus did not undertake, he replied that being omniscient, Jesus had the answer for everything, and did not need to do any research, but lacking that quality of Christ, he had to find the answers for many things by research, either by himself or in partnership with others!

ACKNOWLEDGEMENT

My cordial thanks are due to my beloved wife Susheela for encouraging me to write this book and doing a thorough job of reading the manuscript several times and meticulously spell-checking it before sending it to the printer. My thanks are also due to Rt. Rev. Dr. Isaac Mar Philoxenos Thirumeni for kindly providing the foreword to this book, Binu Samuel Achen and Manoj Idiculla Achen for facilitating the process and the staff of Inspiring Voices for their assistance in the initial publication and the AuthoHouse for this is republication.

REFERENCES

1. Mahabharatha by Ramanarayana Duttta Shastri, 6 volume set, published initially in 1955, by Gorakhpur Gita press, Uttar Pradesh, India. Downloadable from the Internet Archives at: https://openlibrary.org/publishers/Geeta_Press

2. Radhakrishnan, Sarvapalli (1953), The Principal Upanishads, New Delhi: HarperCollins Publishers India (Reprinted in 1994). ISBN 81-7223-124-5. https://archive.org/stream/PrincipalUpanishads/129481965-The-Principal-Upanishads-by-S-Radhakrishnan#page/n5/mode/2up

3. A Dictionary of Creation Myths, David Adams Leeming and Margaret Adams Leeming, Oxford University Press, 1994, Print ISBN-13: 9780195102758

4. Schopenhauer, Arthur; Payne, E. F.J (2000), E. F. J. Payne, ed., Parerga and paralipomena: short philosophical essays, Volume 2 of Parerga and Paralipomena, E. F. J. Payne, Oxford University Press, ISBN 978-0-19-924221-4

5. Sir Monier Monier-Williams, Modern India and the Indians: Being a Series of Impressions, Notes, and Essays, London, Thubner and Co., 1878, Ludgate Hill. https://books.google.com/books?id=se49AAAAMAAJ

6. Forgiver Feted. Christianity Today, Jan 2016, p. 17.

7. E. Stanley Jones, Mahatma Gandhi An Interpretation, Nabu Press (March 13, 2014) ISBN-10: 129382710X, ISBN-13: 978-1293827109

8. Elliott, Elisabeth (1981). Through Gates of Splendor. Wheaton, IL: Tyndale. ISBN 978-0-8423-7151-3

CORRIGENDA
(For the May, 2019 Edition)

Item #	Page #	Line #	Error	Correction
1.	14	4th century	5th century	
2.	14	9	John 4:19	1 John 4:19
3.	22	27	Philippians	Ephesians
4.	30	3	then	the

Printed in the United States
by Baker & Taylor Publisher Services